I0817417

Maria Koran

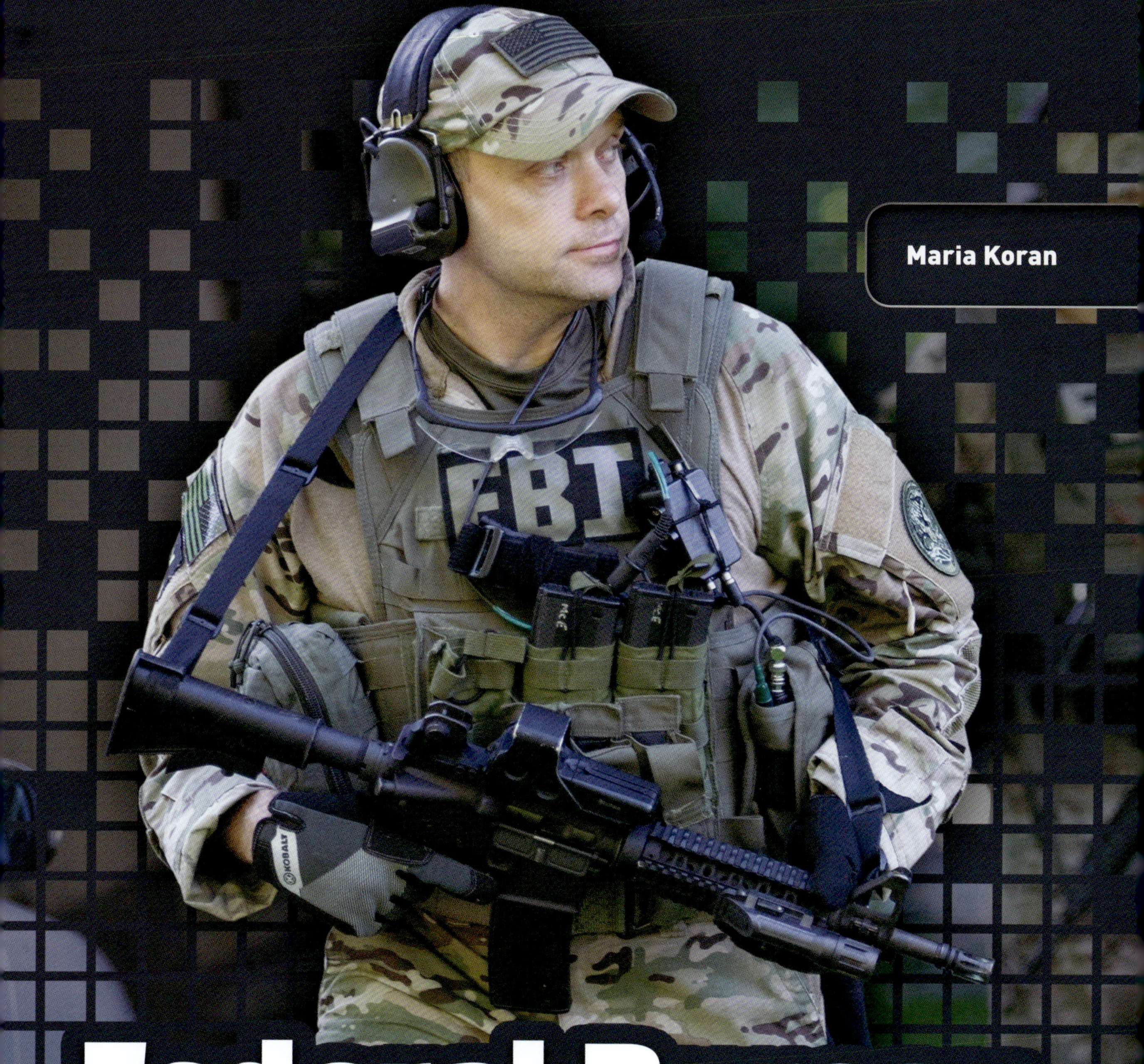

Federal Bureau of Investigation

POWER • AUTHORITY • GOVERNANCE

LIGHTBOX
openlightbox.com

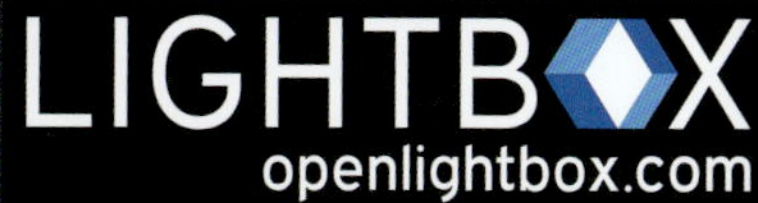

Go to **www.openlightbox.com** and enter this book's unique code.

ACCESS CODE

LBXK5486

Lightbox is an all-inclusive digital solution for the teaching and learning of curriculum topics in an original, groundbreaking way. Lightbox is based on National Curriculum Standards.

STANDARD FEATURES OF LIGHTBOX

AUDIO High-quality narration using text-to-speech system

VIDEOS Embedded high-definition video clips

ACTIVITIES Printable PDFs that can be emailed and graded

WEBLINKS Curated links to external, child-safe resources

SLIDESHOWS Pictorial overviews of key concepts

TRANSPARENCIES Step-by-step layering of maps, diagrams, charts, and timelines

INTERACTIVE MAPS Interactive maps and aerial satellite imagery

QUIZZES Ten multiple choice questions that are automatically graded and emailed for teacher assessment

KEY WORDS Matching key concepts to their definitions

MORE Extra information and details on the subject

FIRST HAND Letters, diaries, and other primary sources

DOCS Speeches, newspaper articles, and other historical documents

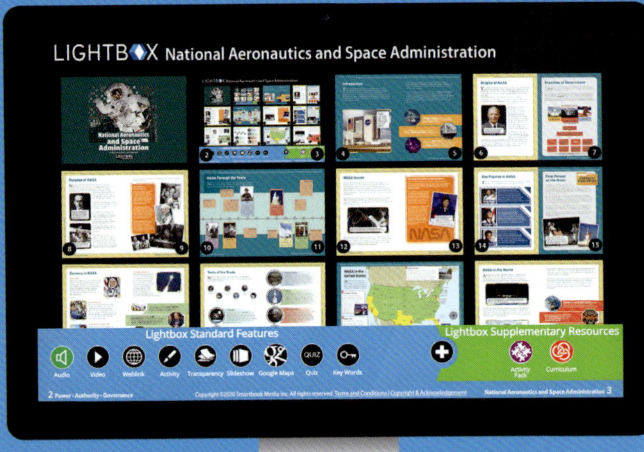

POWER • AUTHORITY • GOVERNANCE

Federal Bureau of Investigation

CONTENTS

Introduction

In the early 1900s, the United States was struggling with crime. In 1908, an organization was created to deal with federal crimes. It became the Federal Bureau of Investigation (FBI).

The FBI is the main law enforcement agency of the federal government. It works under the U.S. Department of Justice (DOJ). The FBI is a federal agency. This means it can investigate and **prosecute** crimes that happen across state lines.

The FBI also provides security for people in the United States. The bureau gathers information that can help prevent crimes. It examines the information and puts it to use. This often involves the FBI working with other countries. When gathering intelligence, the FBI also reports to the U.S. attorney general and the Director of National Intelligencc (DNI).

The FBI has more than 50 offices throughout the United States. The Mobile, Alabama office, established in 1947, is responsible for investigations in southern Alabama and all of the Florida panhandle.

The U.S. government is based on the idea of "popular sovereignty." The people of the country grant power and authority to the government. All parts of the government serve the will of the people. The FBI has great authority and power. However, it must follow certain rules. These rules come from the U.S. Constitution.

The FBI must be careful while investigating and preventing crimes. The bureau must respect individual liberties and civil rights. These rights include the "Right to Privacy." It is guaranteed by the Fourth Amendment to the Constitution.

The DOJ was created in **1789**. In addition to the FBI, it oversees agencies including the Bureau of Alcohol, Tobacco, Firearms, and Explosives (ATF), and the Drug Enforcement Agency (DEA).

The FBI headquarters is the **J. Edgar Hoover building** in Washington, D.C. It was dedicated on **September 30, 1975** by President Gerald R. Ford.

The Bill of Rights is made up of the first **10 amendments** to the U.S. Constitution. They map out the individual rights and freedoms of each citizen of the United States.

Origins of the FBI

At the end of the 18th century, the population of the United States had grown. One of the effects of this growth was an increase in crime. On September 14, 1901, President William McKinley was assassinated. Vice President Theodore Roosevelt became president. Roosevelt wanted to strengthen law enforcement. He appointed Charles J. Bonaparte as his second attorney general to help with this goal.

Theodore Roosevelt was the Police Commissioner of New York City prior to becoming president.

Bonaparte quickly found that he had no agents of his own to investigate crimes. Instead, he had to borrow agents from the Secret Service. Bonaparte realized that he needed his own team. In 1908, he approached Congress with an idea. He wanted to create a special division in the DOJ that had a staff dedicated to investigating crimes.

In June 1908, Bonaparte hired 34 agents for his new department. In a memo dated July 26, 1908, he ordered the new members of his department to report directly to Chief Examiner Stanley W. Finch. Although the department did not have a name yet, this date is considered the founding of the FBI.

In 1909, Bonaparte left his position when Roosevelt left the presidency. On March 16, 1909, George W. Wickersham succeeded him. Wickersham named the new department the Bureau of Investigation (BOI). The name would remain until 1935. That year, the department was renamed as the FBI.

Branches of Government

As part of the DOJ, the FBI reports to the attorney general of the United States. The attorney general reports to the president, who is the head of the executive branch of government.

The U.S. government is organized so that no branch has unlimited authority. This is known as "checks and balances." Although the FBI has a great deal of authority, it is "checked" by both the legislative branch, Congress, and the judicial branch, the U.S. court system.

Congress has the authority to request information from the FBI about topics such as cases or how the bureau is operating. If the FBI does not provide the requested information, the judicial branch is then brought in to enforce these requests.

Purpose of the FBI

The FBI's job is to keep U.S. citizens safe. It protects them from threats and crimes. These threats and crimes take many forms. The FBI must focus on many different areas of law enforcement and intelligence gathering.

Due to work by both the FBI and the U.S. Treasury Department, the gangster Al Capone was convicted and sentenced on October 18, 1931.

The FBI investigates federal crimes. These include organized crime, white-collar crime, and cyber crime. Groups such as the mafia commit organized crimes. There are many different kinds of organized crimes. White-collar crimes are committed by companies or by executives. These crimes often involve money. Computer and internet crimes are cyber crimes. Identity theft is a common cyber crime.

On April 15, 2013, a bomb exploded at the Boston Marathon. The FBI traced the bomb to the Kyrgyz-American brothers Dzhokhar Tsarnaev and Tamerlan Tsarnaev.

The FBI also investigates terrorism. This is the largest threat to national security that the bureau works on. The threat of terrorism is both **domestic** and **international**. Terrorists may be U.S. citizens. However, they may also be from other countries. The FBI uses many tools for **counterintelligence** and **counterterrorism**. The bureau's information sources are often secret. This helps keep the sources safe. However, it also means that people might not find out about acts of terror stopped by the FBI for a long time.

The FBI's job is to provide safety and security for all U.S. citizens. This includes minority communities. Protecting civil rights is an important responsibility of the FBI. The bureau has an entire civil rights division.

The Killing of Medgar Evers

The Constitution guarantees citizens the right to safety and security. Their race or religion does not change this right. The FBI works on civil rights cases. One of these cases was the Medgar Evers case. Evers was a civil rights **activist**. He worked for the National Association for the Advancement of Colored People (NAACP).

Evers was shot on June 12, 1963. The FBI investigated his case for decades. Byron De La Beckwith was eventually convicted of the murder. He was sentenced to life in prison in 1994.

FBI Through the Years

The FBI was created more than 100 years ago. Since then, it has been involved in many major events in U.S. history. Although the agency has changed through the years, it remains an important part of the DOJ.

July 26, 1908
The BOI is founded. Stanley W. Finch is its first director.

April 6, 1917
The United States enters World War I by declaring war on Germany. President Wilson authorizes the BOI to detain **enemy aliens**.

July 1, 1924
The BOI launches the Identification Division. This allows for the exchange of identification records between all cities, counties, and states in the United States.

March 1, 1932
The son of famed pilot Charles Lindbergh is kidnapped. This leads Congress to pass the Federal Kidnapping Act on June 22, 1932.

May 23, 1934
The crime spree of Bonnie Parker and Clyde Barrow ends in a fatal shootout near Sailes, Louisiana.

July 1, 1935
The BOI is renamed as the Federal Bureau of Investigation (FBI).

March 14, 1950
The FBI launches the Ten Most Wanted List. This list encourages citizens of the United States to help the bureau find wanted criminals.

April 5, 1951
Julius and Ethel Rosenberg are convicted of espionage. They provided information on nuclear bombs to the **Soviet Union**.

January 1, 1967
The FBI launches the National Crime Information Center (NCIC). This electronic database can be used by law enforcement from all parts of the United States.

April 4, 1968
Civil rights activist Dr. Martin Luther King, Jr. is murdered in Memphis, Tennessee. The FBI investigates and catches his killer.

February 26, 1993
A bomb explodes at the World Trade Center in New York City. It kills six people and injures more than 1,000. More than 700 FBI agents helped with the investigation.

September 12, 2005
The FBI establishes the National Security Branch (NSB). It combines the bureau's intelligence, counterintelligence, and counterterrorism assets.

June 17, 2013
The FBI names the 500th person to its Ten Most Wanted List.

February 15, 2019
The FBI celebrates the 100th anniversary of its first African American special agent, James Wormley Jones.

FBI Issues

FBI agents put their lives on the line daily to protect the citizens of the United States. However, the organization has also had problems and controversies. Sometimes, the FBI has **infringed** on civil liberties. The agency has also discriminated against women and racial minorities.

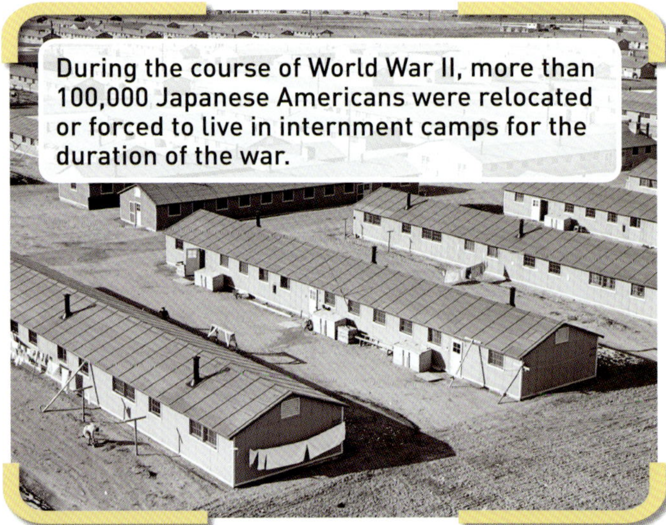
During the course of World War II, more than 100,000 Japanese Americans were relocated or forced to live in internment camps for the duration of the war.

The United States was drawn into World War II when Japan bombed Pearl Harbor in 1941. Within hours of the bombing, the FBI had arrested 1,291 Japanese Americans. The bureau did not have warrants or proof of any criminal acts. These arrests were the first step toward a dark point in American history. Thousands of Japanese Americans were placed in **internment camps** until the war ended.

Although there were women in the FBI in the 1920s, this ended in 1928. The FBI felt that women were not strong enough to become special agents. In 1972, the Equal Opportunity Act was passed. Women were allowed to apply to become special agents. They had to go through the same training as men. That year, 11 women became special agents.

In the 1990s, 30 African Americans sued the FBI for employment discrimination. In 1993, the bureau agreed to make changes. However, the FBI did not follow through. It was taken to court again in 1995. The FBI settled the case again in 2001. It agreed to bring in outside **mediators** to deal with discrimination complaints.

The American Civil Liberties Union

The American Civil Liberties Union (ACLU) is a non-profit organization. The ACLU was founded in the 1920s. It was meant to help protect the freedom of speech guaranteed by the First Amendment. The organization's mission has expanded through the years. Today, it helps protect the civil rights of U.S. citizens.

The ACLU has worked to fight racism against minorities. It also fights against illegal police actions. The ACLU also works to protect the civil rights of citizens in prison.

In the 1960s, the ACLU was involved in the Miranda case. The police had interviewed a suspect without telling him his rights. The ACLU took the case to the Supreme Court. Today, people must be informed of their rights when they are arrested.

ADULT MIRANDA WARNING

1. You have the right to remain silent.
2. Anything you say can and will be used against you in a court of law.
3. You have the right to an attorney.
4. If you cannot afford an attorney, one will be provided for you.

ADULT WAIVER

After the warning and in order to secure a waiver, the following questions should be asked and an affirmative reply secured to each.

1. Do you understand each of these rights I have explained to you?
2. Having these rights in mind, do you wish to talk to us now?

The FBI has learned from its mistakes. Today, it puts a great deal of focus on equality and civil rights. This includes the rights of those that work for the bureau.

Key Figures in the FBI

Many notable people have made their marks while working for the FBI. Some have been field agents. Others helped run the bureau itself.

Stanley W. Finch

Stanley W. Finch (1872 – 1951) was the first director of the BOI. He first joined the DOJ in 1893. Finch helped create the BOI. In 1912, he left the bureau. He worked in different positions in the DOJ before retiring in 1940.

Alaska P. Davidson

Alaska P. Davidson (1868 – 1934) was the first female special agent in the BOI. She was hired on October 11, 1922 at the age of 54. However, when J. Edgar Hoover became director, he said the agency had "no particular work for a woman agent." Davidson was asked to resign. She left the FBI on June 10, 1924.

J. Edgar Hoover

J. Edgar Hoover (1895 – 1972) was the first director of the FBI. He was also the longest-serving director. Under his leadership, the FBI became more like it is today. Hoover oversaw the creation of the first FBI crime lab. He also led the bureau through World War II and the Civil Rights Movement.

J. Edgar Hoover's Handling of Anti-Communism

HISTORICAL CASE STUDY

After World War II, the United States was in conflict with the Soviet Union. The Soviet Union was a communist government country. Spies had given the Soviet Union nuclear secrets. The United States was worried about traitors. Anyone with sympathy toward communism seemed suspicious.

Hoover and the FBI were given broad authority to investigate possible communists. Hoover probed the lives and activities of U.S. citizens. Many U.S. citizens did not know.

In the 1950s, being branded as a communist could cause people to lose their jobs or homes. The FBI investigated many actors, directors, and producers from Hollywood. Some had to defend themselves in front of Congress.

The FBI did stop many potential communist plots against the United States. However, today's FBI or U.S. citizens would not tolerate many of the bureau's acts. Today, they are seen to be violations of civil rights.

Senator Joseph McCarthy was in charge of the Senate hearings regarding U.S. citizens that were potential Communists.

Careers in the FBI

Agents and Special Agents

There are two types of agents in the FBI. The first type can investigate crimes. They do not make arrests. The second type of agent can make arrests. They do not investigate. A "special" agent can do both. There are five Special Agent Entry Programs. Each program has its own requirements.

Intelligence Analyst

The FBI gathers large amounts of information. Intelligence analysts organize and examine this data. They use the information to help solve crimes. Analysts can also help stop crimes from happening. Candidates must pass tests to show they are logical thinkers.

Forensic Accountant

Forensic accountants look at groups that might be involved with crimes. They examine **finances** and the flow of money. Knowing how a criminal was paid can help solve a crime. Candidates need a Certified Public Accountant (CPA) certificate to become a forensic accountant.

Medical and Counseling

Medical emergencies and trauma are often involved with FBI cases. This means that medical and **counseling** personnel are important. FBI medical teams help people at the scenes of violent crimes. Counselors help the survivors of crimes.

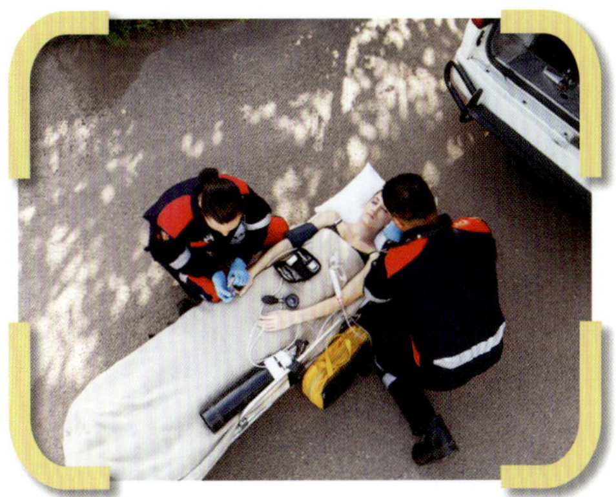

The FBI's budget each year must be approved by Congress. In 2019, the bureau had a budget of approximately **$8.9 billion**.

The director of the FBI is appointed by the president and then confirmed by the U.S. Senate. There is a **10-year limit** to being director of the FBI and an individual can only hold the position once.

STEM stands for Science, Technology, Engineering, and Math. In 2019, the FBI had STEM professionals in all **58** of its field offices.

Tools of the Trade

The FBI requires many different types of tools and devices to do its job. Some of these tools are weapons carried by agents. Others include the advanced systems needed to watch international spy activities.

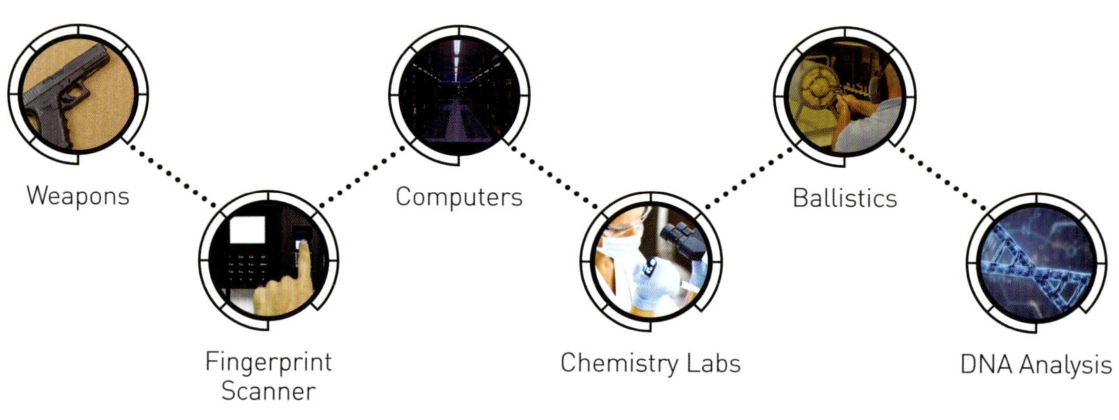

Weapons

The Glock 19M is the standard pistol used by FBI agents. However, agents and FBI **SWAT** teams use other weapons as well. They may use tear gas, shotguns, rifles, or submachine guns. Each weapon is used for a certain situation.

Fingerprint Scanners

Fingerprints are one way that the FBI can identify criminals. No two people have the same fingerprints. The FBI uses two types of scanners. Optical scanners use bright lights. They take a picture of the fingerprint. Capacitive scanners check the difference in height between the "hills and valleys" in the fingerprint.

Computers

The FBI must handle large amounts of information. To do this, they use supercomputers. A supercomputer is an enormous computer. It may fill an entire room. Supercomputers process data millions of times faster than even the fastest laptop.

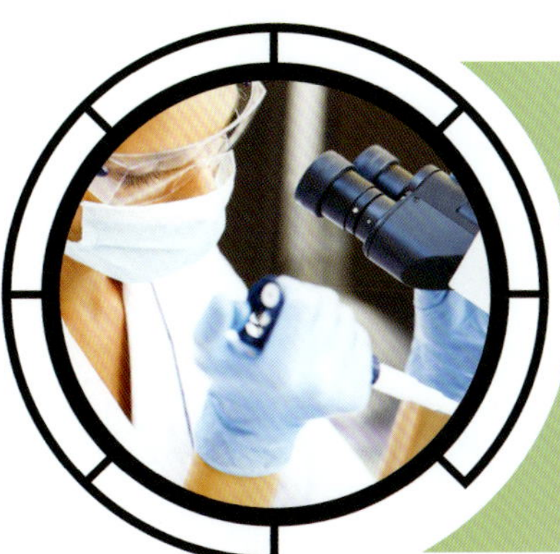

Chemistry Labs

Chemistry is a key part of how many crimes are solved by the FBI. An explosive device may leave **residue**. Paint from a vehicle may be left at a crime scene. Stains may be left on clothing. Identifying these chemicals can help an investigation.

Ballistics

The ballistics lab at the FBI tests weapons. Ballistics analysts can identify what type of gun was used. They can also find out where it was fired. Ballistics may also show how many weapons were used in a crime.

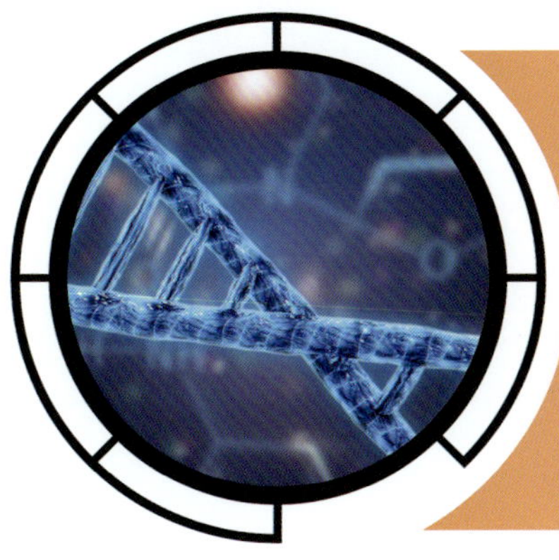

DNA Analysis

One of the most powerful tools used by the FBI is DNA analysis. Deoxyribonucleic acid (DNA) is a molecule that is in all the cells of the human body. The DNA information gathered by the FBI is put into the Combined DNA Index System (CODIS). In addition to helping solve crimes, CODIS is also used throughout the country to help solve missing persons cases.

FBI in the United States

The FBI works across the United States. This means the bureau must work and cooperate with many different agencies and organizations. The FBI works with groups including local law enforcement and the U.S. Marshals Service.

1 Alcatraz Island-San Francisco, California

In the 1960s, Alcatraz Island was the most secure prison in the country. However, John Anglin, Clarence Anglin, and Frank Morris escaped on June 12, 1962. No trace of the three fugitives was ever found. The FBI officially closed the case on December 31, 1979. However, it remains an open case with the U.S. Marshals Service.

2 Oklahoma City, Oklahoma

On April 19, 1995, Timothy McVeigh exploded a bomb in front of the Alfred P. Murrah Federal Building. The explosion killed 168 people, including 19 children. The FBI reviewed nearly a billion pieces of evidence while investigating. McVeigh was convicted on June 2, 1997. The crime remains the largest act of domestic terrorism to date.

Washington, D.C.

In the early 1970s, the Democratic National Committee (DNC) had its headquarters at the Watergate Hotel in Washington, D.C. On June 17, 1972, someone broke into the hotel. The FBI was called in to investigate. The bureau's investigation had far-reaching effects. It led to the **impeachment** of President Richard M. Nixon on February 6, 1974. Nixon resigned from office on August 9, 1974.

Dallas, Texas

On Nov. 22, 1963, President John. F. Kennedy was shot and killed while riding in his **motorcade** in Dallas, Texas. Lee Harvey Oswald was charged with the assassination. However, he was killed by Jack Ruby before he could be prosecuted. There was much speculation that Oswald had accomplices in the crime. However, after years of investigating, the FBI determined that Oswald acted alone.

FBI in the World

Sometimes, the FBI investigates crimes in other countries. The bureau must often work with its **counterpart** in that country. This international cooperation is important. The FBI only has legal authority in the United States. It can only work in another country if that country allows it. This can be very challenging. Other countries may not have the same types of government as the United States. Their law enforcement may also be different.

Pan Am Flight 103 exploded over Lockerbie, Scotland on December 21, 1988. The FBI worked with agencies from many different countries, such as Germany and Great Britain. The international investigation traced the bomb to two agents from Libya. On January 31, 2001, Abdel Basset Ali Al-Megrahi was found guilty of the bombing.

The USS *Cole* was repaired and returned to service in November, 2003. The hallway floor on the ship now features one star for each of the sailors killed.

On October 12, 2000, the USS *Cole* was refueling in Yemen. A small boat next to it exploded. Many sailors were killed or injured. The FBI worked with the Yemeni government to investigate. This cooperation led them to them to the group behind the attack.

In 2015, the FBI made Operation *Shrouded Horizon* public. This operation had targeted a secret online forum known as "Darkode." It was used by cyber criminals. The FBI worked with agencies in 19 other countries in its investigation.

The governments of the world understand the need for law enforcement cooperation. They have created organizations to help countries work together. The International Criminal Police Organization (Interpol) helps agencies share information. Countries can also take legal issues to the International Court of Justice (ICJ) at The Hague, Netherlands.

The headquarters of Interpol is located at Lyon, France.

Pieces of **Pan Am Flight 103** landed over **845** square miles in Scotland.

17 sailors were killed on the **USS *Cole*.**

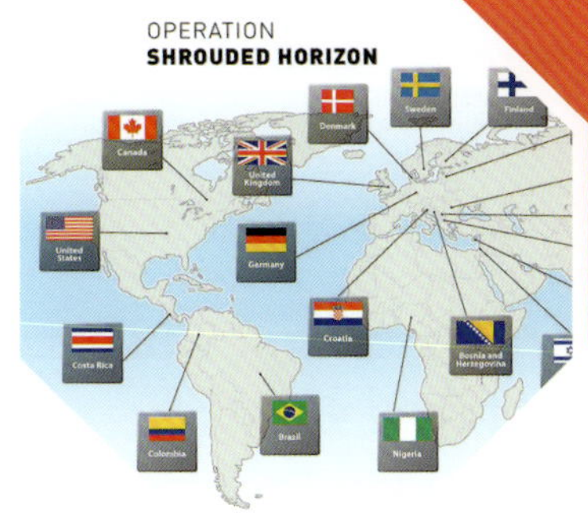

Operation Shrouded Horizon resulted in arrests in 20 countries and indictments against **12 U.S. citizens**.

FBI Today

The FBI works to keep up with a changing world. New technology causes many challenges for today's FBI. People use many different tools to communicate. Social media provides the FBI with both challenges and opportunities.

The 9/11 attacks made counterterrorism a top FBI priority. The bureau works to protect U.S. citizens from physical terror attacks. It also tries to stop cyber terror attacks. However, this job can be difficult. Modern computers are fast. Their codes are complex. People use hundreds of different ways to talk to each other. Technology also makes it much easier for people to commit other crimes. This includes political corruption, corporate crime, and cyber crimes. These crimes are also part of the FBI's responsibilities. The FBI must be sure that it has up-to-date technology and training.

The FBI Cyber Division is responsible for investigating and prosecuting internet crimes such as cyber fraud.

Social media can help the FBI identify people that might be a threat to the United States. Online groups and forums exist for the purpose of organizing terror attacks or committing crimes. However, the FBI must not overreach its authority and infringe on the privacy of U.S. citizens. The FBI must balance its authority against the civil rights of the citizens it protects.

9/11

MODERN CASE STUDY

On September 11, 2001, the Al-Qaeda terror group hijacked four airliners. Two were flown into the World Trade Center in New York City. Both towers were destroyed. A third plane hit The Pentagon in Washington, D.C. The fourth plane crashed in a field near Shanksville, Pennsylvania. The passengers had overpowered the hijackers.

The cleanup and recovery efforts at Ground Zero in New York took almost nine months to complete.

The attack was the largest act of terrorism in history. It caused the death of 2,996 people. More than 6,000 were injured. The investigation took thousands of people from all over the world. It cost millions of dollars and took years to complete.

The 9/11 attacks changed how government agencies share information. It also affected how the FBI investigates terrorism. The United States passed the Patriot Act after the attack. It gave government departments more authority. They could examine the activities and communications of U.S. citizens. The act was weakened in 2015. However, it is still controversial. Some people feel it goes against their right to privacy. It also goes against their freedom from illegal searches and seizures. These are both guaranteed by the Fourth Amendment.

The Pentagon is the headquarters of the U.S. Department of Defense.

FBI Looking to the Future

Today's FBI must plan for tomorrow's crimes and threats. This planning can be difficult. Both technology and U.S. culture are changing.

Soon, "**quantum computing**" will change computers and how fast they work. People now have watches that put their computer screen on their wrist. People are now even putting computer chips under their skin for work. Today, people live in a cyber world. It is changing faster every day. This is the ever-evolving technology that the FBI must plan for and be ready to use in the future. In 2019, the FBI listed 11 areas of focus. These included cyber capabilities and information technology.

The FBI is the lead federal agency for investigating cyber attacks by terrorists, hostile nations, and criminals.

In 2008, the National Cyber Investigative Joint Task Force (NCIJTF) was established to combat the country's sophisticated cyber threats. The NCIJTF is made up of more than 20 government agencies including the FBI, Department of Homeland Security, National Security Agency, and more.

Changes are also happening in U.S. society. Many people use social media. The country's racial demographics are also changing. This is causing a shift in the way that people view the roles, rights, and responsibilities of the three branches of government. The FBI is given its authority by the people of the United States. This means the job of the FBI will change as the culture of the United States changes. One of the FBI's 2019 goals was to improve the bureau's openness. The FBI is also working to increase its diversity. In 2019, nearly 70 percent of special agents were Caucasian men. By using tools such as social media, the FBI hopes to encourage more people to apply. The FBI must be sure it can do its job to keep the citizens of the United States safe and secure.

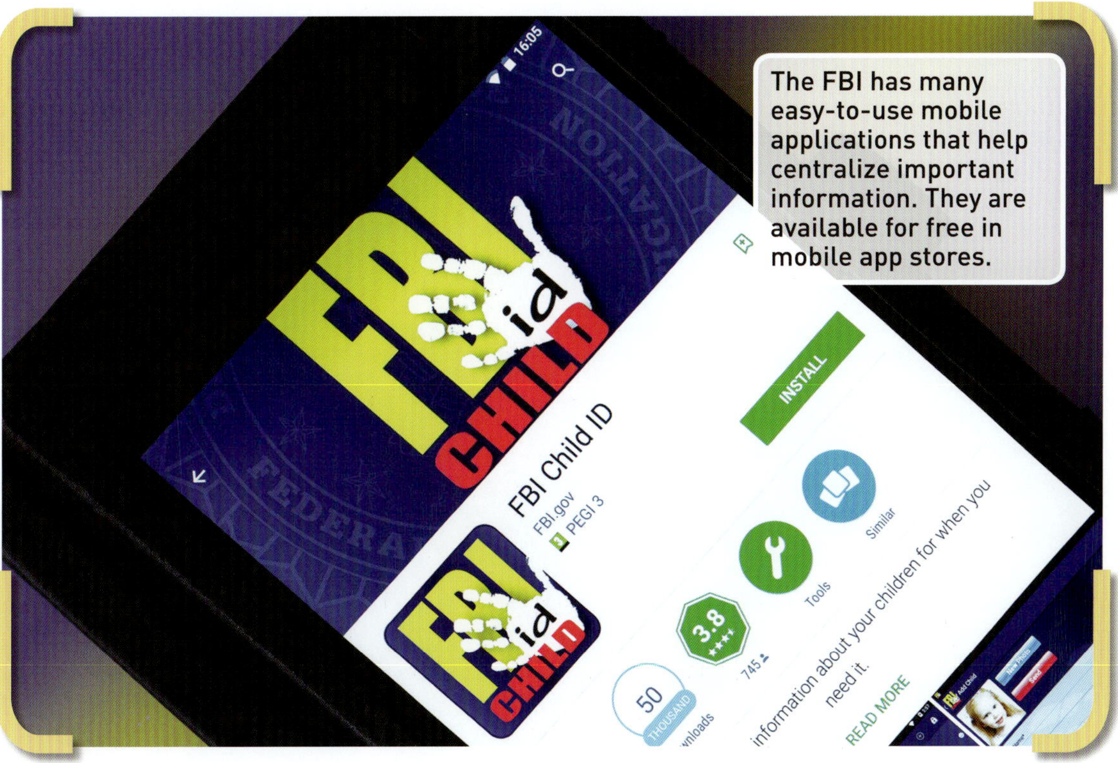

The FBI has many easy-to-use mobile applications that help centralize important information. They are available for free in mobile app stores.

ACTIVITY

Create a Policy Paper

Rather than just solving a crime after it happens, the FBI tries to stop it from happening in the first place. To help with crime prevention, the FBI monitors social media sites. These include Facebook, Instagram, Snapchat, and Twitter.

The freedoms and rights guaranteed by the Bill of Rights are extremely important to U.S. citizens. One of these rights is the Freedom of Speech guaranteed by the First Amendment. Another is the Right to Privacy guaranteed by the Fourth Amendment.

Develop your own opinion on social media, the First Amendment, and law enforcement. Write a policy paper that summarizes your opinion.

Step 1:

Answer the following questions to help you develop your opinion.

1. Are there any words that you should not be able to use on social media? If so, why should they be banned?
2. Are there any topics that you should not be allowed to talk about on social media? If so, why should they be banned?
3. If one of these words or topics is used on social media, how do you think the social media site should handle it?
4. When should law enforcement be allowed to watch people or their computers?
5. Are there any topics or conversations on social media that should immediately involve law enforcement?
6. What types of social media topics or conversations should cause online communications to be watched? Which ones should cause law enforcement to visit people in person?
7. Should law enforcement be able to take someone's computer or ban them from the internet?

Step 2:

Take your opinions from Questions 1 – 7 and write a one-page policy paper. This should explain the policy you think would work to balance social media freedom of speech and law enforcement. Include an introductory paragraph to explain your policy.

- Paragraph 1: What is the problem?
- Paragraph 2: What steps can solve the problem?
- Paragraph 3: Which step do you think should be taken? Why?

QUIZ ★★

1 What are the three branches of government in the United States?

2 What are the first ten amendments to the Constitution called?

3 What is the name of the principle by which a government is given its power by the people of the country?

4 Who was the first director of the Federal Bureau of Investigation?

5 Which amendment to the Constitution guarantees citizens freedom of speech?

6 In what year did the FBI launch its Ten Most Wanted list?

7 How long may an FBI director serve before they must leave the position?

8 What is the name of the system that contains all of the DNA information gathered by the FBI?

9 The Department of Justice is a division of what branch of the U.S. government?

10 What are three possible FBI careers?

ANSWERS

1. Executive, Legislative, and Judicial **2.** The Bill of Rights **3.** Popular sovereignty **4.** J. Edgar Hoover **5.** The First Amendment **6.** 1950 **7.** Ten years **8.** Combined DNA Index System (CODIS) **9.** Executive **10.** Agents and special agents, intelligence analyst, forensic accountant, or medical and counseling

KEY WORDS

activist: one who strongly supports a cause

counseling: meeting and talking regularly with someone who can give advice

counterintelligence: a program of a government or other organization to frustrate enemy espionage

counterterrorism: actions taken to combat and prevent terrorism

counterpart: equal

domestic: of the country one is in

enemy aliens: people living in a country with whom their home country is in conflict

finances: the money owned by a person, bank, or government

impeachment: the presentation of formal charges against a public official

infringed: violated or gone beyond the limits of

international: of or having to do with what happens between two or more countries

internment camps: camps that play the role of a low security prison

mediators: people who act as a go-between for two groups or individuals

motorcade: a parade of motor vehicles

prosecute: to begin a court action against in order to enforce the law

quantum computing: computers that use processors based on the properties of atoms and molecules

residue: a substance or quantity that remains after a part has been removed

Soviet Union: A country that no longer exists that was made up of 15 republics in eastern Europe and northern Asia.

SWAT: Special Weapons and Tactics

INDEX

LIGHTBOX

SUPPLEMENTARY RESOURCES

Click on the plus icon found in the bottom left corner of each spread to open additional teacher resources.

- Download and print the book's quizzes and activities
- Access curriculum correlations
- Explore additional web applications that enhance the Lightbox experience

LIGHTBOX DIGITAL TITLES
Packed full of integrated media

VIDEOS

INTERACTIVE MAPS

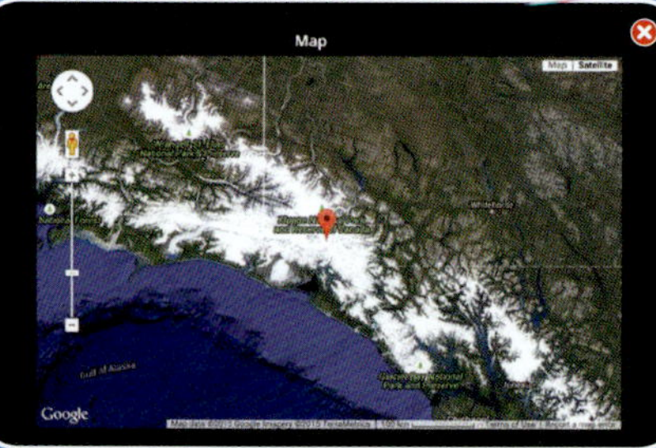

WEBLINKS

SLIDESHOWS

QUIZZES

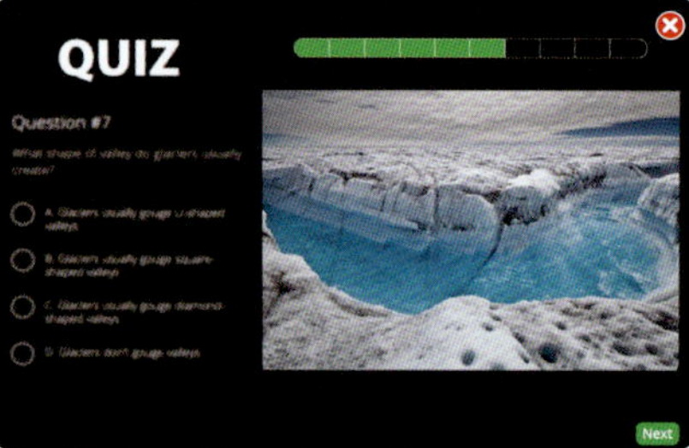

OPTIMIZED FOR

- ✔ TABLETS
- ✔ WHITEBOARDS
- ✔ COMPUTERS
- ✔ AND MUCH MORE!

Published by Smartbook Media Inc.
350 5th Avenue, 59th Floor New York, NY 10118
Website: www.openlightbox.com

Library of Congress Control Number: 2019939796

ISBN 978-1-5105-4689-9 (hardcover)
ISBN 978-1-5105-4690-5 (multi-user eBook)

Printed in Guangzhou, China
1 2 3 4 5 6 7 8 9 0 23 22 21 20 19

052019
122718

Editor: John Willis
Art Director: Terry Paulhus

Every reasonable effort has been made to trace ownership and to obtain permission to reprint copyright material. The publisher would be pleased to have any errors or omissions brought to its attention so that they may be corrected in subsequent printings.

The publisher acknowledges Alamy, Shutterstock, and Wikimedia Commons as its primary image suppliers for this title.